AMERICAN EXCEPTIONALISM

An Experiment in History

AMERICAN EXCEPTIONALISM

An Experiment in History

Charles Murray

AEI Press

Washington, D.C.

Distributed by arrangement with the Rowman & Littlefield Publishing Group, 4501 Forbes Boulevard, Suite 200, Lanham, MD 20706. To order call toll free 1-800-462-6420 or 1-717-794-3800.

For all other inquiries please contact AEI Press, 1150 17th Street, N.W., Washington, D.C. 20036 or call 1-800-862-5801.

Murray, Charles A.
  American exceptionalism : an experiment in history / Charles Murray.
    pages cm
  Includes bibliographical references.
  ISBN 978-0-8447-7264-6 (pbk.) -- ISBN 0-8447-7264-X (pbk.)
  ISBN 978-0-8447-7265-3 (ebook) -- ISBN 0-8447-7265-8 (ebook)
  1. Exceptionalism--United States--History.
  2. National characteristics, American--History. I. Title.
  E169.1M963 2013
  305.800973--dc23

CONTENTS

1

INTRODUCTION

It is April 30, 1789, a sunny spring day, and you are a European who has traveled to New York to see the inauguration of George Washington as the first president of the United States.

Standing in the crowd in front of Federal Hall on Wall Street, you are watching the beginning of an experiment in governance unlike any in the history of the world. Four million people, spread out over thirteen colonies stretching from New England to Georgia, have separated themselves from the world's greatest power and then invented a new nation from scratch. That all by itself makes the United States unique and also makes it impossible to predict what might happen next.

It isn't just the newness of the nation that makes its future so imponderable. The Americans could easily have chosen familiar institutions. If George Washington had been declared king of the United States, the Founding Fathers given hereditary titles, and a deliberative body created as a counterweight to the king's powers, you would have had a European framework to help you think through the new nation's prospects. But instead the founders of the United States have created a form of government that will attempt all sorts of things that are widely thought to be impossible.

Republican government itself is widely thought to be impracticable and unstable. No country in continental Europe has a constitutional monarchy, let alone a republic in which all power ultimately resides in the citizens. Even Britain, Europe's most politically liberal nation, still expects the sovereign to play a major role in the governance of the nation and shudders at the memory of its own brief experiment as a republic.

It is widely thought to be impossible for a nation to function with a head of state elected for a limited term. How can the Americans realistically expect a successful, popular president who is chief executive, head of state, and commander-in-chief of the nation's armed forces to retire voluntarily? Every lesson of history teaches that transmission of power through an electoral system doesn't work for long.

Surely it is impossible that a piece of paper, the Constitution, can command the allegiance— indeed, the reverence—that the American system will require. The consensus at the Constitutional Convention and in the debates over ratification of the Constitution is that the new Supreme Court has the power to strike down laws already passed by the legislature and implemented by the executive power— an unprecedented level of judicial independence.[1]

Most stunning of all, you are watching the first nation in the world translate an ideology of individual liberty into a governing creed. As an educated European of the eighteenth century, you are familiar with the ideology itself as expressed by John Locke and other writers of the Enlightenment. But philosophy is one thing. It is quite another to restrict the power of the central government as radically as the new American Constitution does.

Your imaginary self at the inauguration of George Washington had many real counterparts in the early decades of our history. A long line of Europeans—most famously Alexis de Tocqueville, but also widely read observers such as Harriet Martineau, Frances Trollope, and Charles Dickens, plus thousands of other lesser-known visitors—wrote books, letters, and journals describing the Americans to their fellow countrymen. They often had the tone of a zoologist writing about a hitherto unknown species. For whatever else these observers might say about the United States, they all agreed on one thing: the United States was quite unlike their own or any other nation. It was exceptional.

The concept of American exceptionalism has been used in many ways. Some have interpreted "exceptional" to mean "wonderful," and American exceptionalism has been used as a framework for describing whatever the proponent thinks is wonderful America.[2] It has been interpreted to mean that America has a special mission in the world and used in support of whatever measures that

> *"For whatever else these observers might say about the United States, they all agreed on one thing: the United States was quite unlike their own or any other nation. It was exceptional."*

mission is taken to imply.[3] Those who don't like the idea of American exceptionalism have attempted to refute it by pointing to the ways in which the history of the United States parallels that of other great imperial powers, arguing that the United States has the same awful defects as other empires.[4]

So the concept of American exceptionalism has become associated with meanings that are filled with emotion and value judgments—intertwined with patriotism, for those who approve of it, or connoting jingoism or chauvinism, for those who disapprove. I write about American exceptionalism from another tradition that has four characteristics:

American exceptionalism is a concept that was shared by observers throughout the Western world, not just Americans. The Founders certainly believed that they were creating something of extraordinary significance. That's why the motto on the Great Seal of the United States is *novus ordo seclorum*—"a new order of the ages." But it was foreigners who took the lead in describing the United States and Americans as being unlike all other countries and peoples.

American exceptionalism does not imply American excellence or superiority. Americans tend to think that most of the traits of American exceptionalism are positive, but others, especially European elites, have always disagreed. Even those of us who think they are positive must acknowledge aspects of American exceptionalism that are problematic.

American exceptionalism is a fact of America's past, not something that you can choose whether to "believe in" any more than you can choose whether to "believe in" the battle of Gettysburg. Understanding its meaning is indispensable for anyone who wants to understand what it has meant to be an American.

American exceptionalism refers to qualities that were first observed in the opening century of our history. There's no reason why they necessarily still apply today. The extent to which they still apply is an empirical question.

2

THE ELEMENTS OF AMERICAN EXCEPTIONALISM

America in the nineteenth century was exceptional in many ways, and there is no uniquely right way to group them. My choice has been to group them under these four headings: America as a geographic setting, American ideology, traits of the American people, and the operation of the American political system.

AN EXCEPTIONAL SETTING

Most nineteenth-century foreigners and modern scholars have ascribed the unusual traits of Americans to our ideology and political system. But when the country began, the Founders were unanimously of the opinion that their creation could work in practice only because of qualities that already existed in the American people—their honesty, industriousness, religiosity, and morality, to name four that all of the Founders discussed in one way or another.[5]

These qualities were in turn fostered by the American setting. For one thing, the way to America lay across the North Atlantic. What kind of people were likely to accept the hazards and hardships of that crossing? For another, America in the sixteenth and early seventeenth centuries consisted of a handful of small cities and tiny hamlets dotting a wilderness. What kind of people were eager for the opportunity to farm the thin, rocky soil of New England or, farther south, to chop down a forest and root out the stumps before they could plow their first field? What kind of people were willing to cross the ocean, chop down the forest, and, after all that, were prepared to subsist with hardly any access to either the necessities or comforts of life that weren't grown, gathered, shot, bred, spun, woven, salted, churned, milled, distilled, quarried, hewn, and constructed by their own families?

The answer is that such people tended to be courageous, honest, incredibly hardworking, and to belong to close-knit families. The pre-Revolutionary American setting rigorously selected immigrants to have many of the qualities that the Founders depended upon to make the Constitution work.

America's geographic setting had other exceptional aspects. From the beginning, the United States enjoyed the buffer of the Atlantic Ocean. In Thomas Jefferson's words, we were "kindly separated by nature and a wide ocean from the exterminating havoc of one quarter of the globe."[6] After the War of 1812, the combination of that buffer and having peaceable neighbors to the north and south meant that the United States could ignore problems of military preparedness and diplomacy that preoccupied European governments.

> *"From the beginning, the masses—first in Europe, later in Asia, and finally in Africa and Latin America—have thought of America as the land of opportunity and flocked to America by the millions."*

After the nation expanded over the Appalachians, then added vast new lands west of the Mississippi through the Louisiana Purchase, the United States acquired another advantage. Those lands to the west included vast tracts of the richest soil in the world, much of it on open plains that required only a plow and a strong horse to convert into prosperous farms. Americans who needed a fresh start or who just wanted to try something new had a ready option: pull up stakes and move west. That same open frontier meant that many of the tensions of immigration were dampened. Established citizens and new immigrants need not compete for land in crowded countrysides. There was plenty of room to spread out.

In 1893, historian Frederick Jackson Turner extended such observations into a full-blown theory of American exceptionalism, arguing that the American identity evolved because of the existence of a frontier. It fostered a composite nationality for the American people: "In the crucible of the frontier the immigrants were Americanized, liberated, and fused into a mixed race, English in neither nationality nor characteristics."[7] The needs of the pioneers for manufactured goods from the East Coast fostered the growth of the nation's transportation infrastructure, including roads, canals, and later railways, which bound the nation together. Most importantly, in Turner's view, the frontier promoted the rugged individualism of which Americans were so proud:

> The result is that to the frontier the American intellect owes its striking characteristics. That coarseness and strength combined with acuteness and inquisitiveness; that practical, inventive turn of mind, quick to find expedients; that masterful grasp of material things, lacking in the artistic but powerful to effect great ends; that restless, nervous energy, that dominant individualism, working for good and for evil, and withal that buoyancy and exuberance which comes with freedom—these are traits of the frontier,

or traits called out elsewhere because of the existence of the frontier.[8]

Turner's thesis was highly influential through the 1950s, for the same reason that movie Westerns at that time exalted the relationship between the frontier and American individualism. Among Americans in the first half of the twentieth century, both Turner's thesis and the Westerns corresponded with a shared perception of our history.

AN EXCEPTIONAL IDEOLOGY

"It has been our fate as a nation not to have ideologies, but to be one," historian Richard Hofstadter once observed.[9] Unlike any previous political system in history, ours implements a specific set of philosophical ideas about the nature of human beings.

The Founders began with the assumption that human beings possess natural rights that cannot be given or withheld by the state, but are every person's birthright. That famous sentence from the Declaration of Independence—"We hold these truths to be self-evident, that all men are created equal, that they are endowed by their creator with certain unalienable rights; that among these are life, liberty, and the pursuit of happiness"—was not a rhetorical flourish. It was "an expression of the

American mind," as Thomas Jefferson wrote almost fifty years later, and it distilled into thirty-five words the ideology that the Revolution sought to realize.[10]

What was the nature of the human clay they had to work with? On the optimistic side, the Founders accepted that human beings were naturally fitted for society.[11] Some, such as Thomas Jefferson, thought that human beings have an inherent moral sense. Others, such as John Adams, thought that human beings naturally seek the approbation of those around them, and this impulse can be used to induce their good behavior. The Founders also were optimistic about human potential. They believed that virtue and intelligence could be found not only among the elite but in anyone. They also believed that everyone may aspire to happiness. In a world that had taken for granted that virtue and meaningful happiness could be achieved only by the superior few, this view of human potential was novel and radical.

On the pessimistic side, the Founders were equally convinced that men behave problematically in the political arena. As James Madison explained in *Federalist 10*, human beings pursue power and, in its pursuit, form factions, which he defined as "a number of citizens...who are united and actuated by some common impulse of passion, or of interest, adverse to the rights of other citizens, or to the permanent and aggregate interests of the community." The historical experience of all previous republics demonstrated that factions eventually strangle freedom and destroy republics. And no wonder. The power that only a government can legitimately wield—the power of compelling obedience, by force if necessary—is such a potent force for advancing one's own interests that some people will do almost anything to achieve that power. As factions cannot be prevented, the only thing that government can do is limit their evil effects. "If men were angels," Madison wrote in one of the most famous passages from *The Federalist*, "no government would be necessary. . . . In framing a government which is to be administered by men over men, the great difficulty lies in this: you must first enable the government to control the governed; and in the next place oblige it to control itself."[12]

Thus the twin assumptions of the American system. Deprived of the use of force (a crucial caveat), human beings acting in their private capacity tend to be resourceful and benign. Human beings acting in the political realm tend to be resourceful and dangerous. If you ever find yourself thinking that philosophy doesn't matter, consider the power of this pair of views about human nature in shaping the American polity. The understanding I have just described motivated the Constitution's elaborate system of checks and balances and the Bill of Rights' even more explicit constraints on government's innate tendency to expand beyond its proper role. From this understanding flowed not only the structure of the American government but a shared creed, or political religion, or civic culture—it has been called all of those things.

What I want to emphasize, because it cannot be obvious to twenty-first-century readers, is how thoroughly and broadly this ideology was understood by the American public. Perhaps a specific illustration will help. One of the key tenets of the American ideology was that human beings acting in their own best interest will also serve the public good—that's why freedom works in practice. The basis for that idea came from many thinkers, but chief among them was Adam Smith through his seminal pair of books, *The Theory of Moral Sentiments* and *The Wealth of Nations*. Smith's famous concept of the "invisible hand" in economic transactions that leads people who are pursuing their own profit to benefit others as well is part of that argument. Tocqueville originated an excellent phrase for labeling the argument: "self-interest rightly understood."

Smith's work became influential throughout Europe in promoting capitalism and free markets. In the United States, self-interest rightly understood became the basis for the defense of freedom. Making that defense was not confined to intellectuals in the universities or to political theorists. It was an idea that permeated the nation. The doctrine of self-interest rightly understood "finds universal acceptance [in America]," Tocqueville wrote. "You may trace it at the bottom of all their actions, you will remark it in all they say. It is as often asserted by the poor man as by the rich." In fact, they believed it so emphatically that, in Tocqueville's view, they undersold their native generosity:

> The Americans . . . are fond of explaining almost all the actions of their lives by the principle of self-interest rightly understood; they show with complacency how an enlightened regard for themselves constantly prompts them to assist one another and inclines them willingly to sacrifice a portion of their time and property to the welfare of the state. In this respect I think they frequently fail to do themselves justice, for in the United States as well as elsewhere people are sometimes seen to give way to those disinterested and spontaneous impulses that are natural to man; but the Americans seldom admit that they yield to emotions of this kind; they are more anxious to do honor to their philosophy than to themselves.[13]

That's just one example of what it's like to live in a country based on a common ideology. Historian Bernard Bailyn has eloquently conveyed Americans' enthusiasm for that ideology at the dawn of the United States:

> The details of this new world were not as yet clearly depicted; but faith ran high that a better world than any that had ever been known could be built where authority was distrusted and held in constant scrutiny; where the status of men flowed from their achievements and from their personal qualities, not from distinctions ascribed to them at birth; and where the use of power over the lives of men was jealously guarded and severely restricted. It was only where there was this defiance, this refusal to truckle, this distrust of all authority, political or social, that institutions could express human aspirations, not crush them.[14]

It was a truly exceptional way for a people to see themselves in relationship to their government.

EXCEPTIONAL TRAITS

What made America exceptional in practice was its civic culture. Daily life was different in America

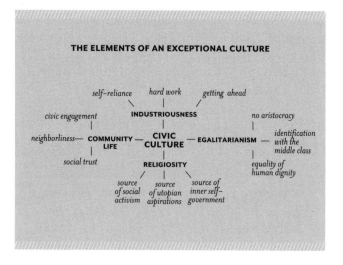

THE ELEMENTS OF AN EXCEPTIONAL CULTURE

from daily life in Europe. Four American traits were central to the evolution of that culture: industriousness, egalitarianism, religiosity, and an amalgam of philanthropy and volunteerism that was uniquely American.

Industriousness. The word the Founders used was *industry*, but the meaning of the modern version, *industriousness*, is close enough for our purposes. Daily hard work was the lot of ordinary people everywhere in the world when America was founded, but *industriousness* means something more than working hard. It signifies the bone-deep American assumption that life is to be spent getting ahead through hard work and thereby making a better life for oneself and one's children.

The industriousness of Americans fascinated the rest of the world. No other American quality was so consistently seen as exceptional. Francis Grund, a German observer who wrote at about the same time as Tocqueville, put it in words that were echoed by many other European visitors:

> Active occupation is not only the principal source of [the Americans'] happiness, and the foundation of their natural greatness, but they are absolutely wretched without it.... It is the very soul of an American; he pursues it, not as a means of procuring for himself and his family the necessary comforts of life, but as the fountain of all human felicity.[15]

Underlying the willingness to do the work was the abundance of opportunity that America offered as a lure, and it affected people in every class. Henry Adams pointed out that it affected those on the bottom of American society more powerfully than those on top.

> Reversing the old-world system, the American stimulant increased in energy

as it reached the lowest and most ignorant class, dragging and whirling them upward as in the blast of a furnace. The penniless and homeless Scotch or Irish immigrant was caught and consumed by it; for every stroke of the axe and the hoe made him a capitalist, and made gentlemen of his children. . . . The instinct of activity, once created, seemed heritable and permanent in the race.[16]

Not all European visitors thought American industriousness so very admirable, because it was closely linked with what they saw as an undesirable obsession with money. "Mammon has no more zealous worshipper than your true Yankee," one English visitor wrote. "His homage is not merely that of the lip, or of the knee; it is an entire prostration of the heart; the devotion of all powers, bodily and mental, to the service of the idol."[17]

Another aspect of this American trait was a fierce determination to be economically independent—what became known over the course of the nineteenth century as self-reliance and later as rugged individualism. Francis Grund wrote that during a decade of life in the United States in the 1820s and 1830s, "I have never known a native American to ask for charity. . . . An American, embarrassed by his pecuniary circumstances, can hardly be prevailed upon to ask or accept the assistance of his own relations; and will, in many instances, scorn to have recourse to his own parents."[18]

Egalitarianism. Today, egalitarianism is associated with the Left and with policies that seek to equalize outcomes. The egalitarianism of nineteenth-century America had nothing to do with equality of outcomes but with equality of human dignity. One of the things that Europeans noticed first about America was the absence of the paraphernalia of class. For example, no aristocracy meant no labels for different social levels—no sequence of social stations going from commoner to knight to baronet to earl to marquis to duke to prince—and no honorifics such as "your excellency," "my lord," or "your grace" to go with those labels. Americans of a lower status did not bow, or take off their hats, or tug their forelocks to Americans of a higher status. Affluent Americans wore better clothes than people without much money, but there were no distinctive modes of dress that let people know just by looking at them to what class people belonged. Your accent did not stamp your class. Some of the tiny proportion of nineteenth-century Americans with college educations could be recognized by the way they talked (the Harvard accent was especially notorious), but the people who talked that way were more likely to be ridiculed than respected by the rest of America.

In the nineteenth-century America that Tocqueville saw, those of higher status also refused to play the part they would be expected to play in Europe. "In the United States, the more opulent citizens take great care not to stand aloof from the people," Tocqueville wrote. "On the contrary, they constantly keep on easy terms with the lower classes: they listen to them, they speak to them every day."[19] Part of the reason they did so was that they didn't want others to think they held themselves to be better than anyone else. In the American vernacular, it was known as getting too big for your britches and meant that you needed taking down a peg. The snobbish Easterner who visits the hinterlands and is outwitted by the locals became a standard feature of American popular literature and theatre. By the same token, Americans didn't like the idea of a lower class, except for people who earned it. So Americans had invidious names for people with lower-class behavior—"white trash" and the like—but not for people who were simply poor but otherwise respectable.

And so it came to be that when pollsters in the twentieth century first began to ask Americans what class they were in, it was discovered that almost everybody said they were working class or middle class. A great many poor Americans refused to consider themselves lower class, and a great many

> *"America was by no means a classless society, but Americans retained a strong sense that whatever class you were in was a matter of what you had made of yourself, not who your family was, and an equally strong sense that richer does not mean more virtuous or of greater human worth."*

rich Americans refused to consider themselves upper class. America was by no means a classless society, but Americans retained a strong sense that whatever class you were in was a matter of what you had made of yourself, not who your family was, and an equally strong sense that richer does not mean more virtuous or of greater human worth. No country in Europe at the time had a social system remotely like it.

Religiosity. Ironically, given the importance they placed on religion, few of the Founders were themselves traditionally devout. They were men of the Enlightenment and its skepticism. Some, like Jefferson, were explicitly deists; others, like Washington, attended church but were vague about their belief in the details of Christian doctrine. But they emphatically agreed that religion was essential to the success of the American experiment. John Adams put it most evocatively:

> We have no government armed with power capable of contending with human passions unbridled by morality and religion. Avarice, ambition, revenge, or gallantry, would break the strongest cords of our Constitution as a whale goes through a net. Our Constitution was made only for a moral and religious people. It is wholly inadequate to the government of any other.[20]

And a religious people we were, in ways that once again had no counterpart in Europe. Religion was still widely practiced in Europe at the time of the Revolution and throughout the nineteenth century, but it was invariably entangled with nationalism and the state. Virtually all European countries had a state-sponsored religion that received special legal standing and often direct financial subsidies. The United States was unique in the unqualified breadth of its religious freedom and in the absence of any state assistance for a preferred faith, both explicitly protected by the first amendment of the Bill of Rights.

That absence of government support for American religiosity has arguably been its salvation. Unlike their European counterparts, American churches have had to compete in the marketplace for adherents, and the result throughout our history has been a riotous variety of religions, many of them completely new sects. Furthermore, the most vital churches have also been the ones that have espoused the central Christian doctrines most enthusiastically. Thomas Jefferson was right about many things, but spectacularly wrong when he wrote that, "I trust that there is not a young man now living in the United States who will not die an Unitarian."[21]

Unlike Europe, where the practice of religion not only retreated over the nineteenth century but became more formalistic as well, devout Christian faith persisted undiminished in the United States. The depth and passion of American religion had a huge impact on secular society. Many eminent social scientists have attributed much of America's course to the Protestant religious traditions that began with the Pilgrims and the Mayflower. For sociologist Robert Bellah, the Christian belief in the second coming of Christ was a crucial element.[22] For political scientist Samuel Huntington, the powerful strain of religious dissent in the American tradition was "the original source both of the close intermingling of religion and politics that [has] characterized subsequent American history and of the moral passion that has powered the engines of political change in America."[23] For Catholic philosopher Michael Novak, the dissenters of Europe who became the Baptists, Quakers, Presbyterians, and Methodists of America had a distinctive vision of god as "'Spirit and Truth,' whose main interest in creating humans on earth was their advancement in liberty—outer liberty in their common political life, and inner liberty in their consciences."[24] For sociologist Martin Lipset, the Protestant heritage explains why "Americans are utopian moralists who press hard to institutionalize virtue, destroy evil people, and eliminate wicked institutions and practices."[25]

These forces were exemplified by the periodic religious "Great Awakenings" that economic historian and Nobel laureate Robert Fogel has described.[26] The first Great Awakening occurred in the first half of the eighteenth century and was instrumental in fostering forces that led to the Revolution. The second Great Awakening began in the early 1800s and lasted until around 1840, bringing with it the temperance movement, support for universal elementary education, and abolitionism. The third Great Awakening is variously said to have started between the 1860s and 1890; it continued into the early 1900s and laid the ethical basis for the emancipation of women, the reforms of the New Deal and, later, the civil rights movement. Widely held and deeply felt religious beliefs of such strength that they shaped public policy were phenomena alien to Europe's experience during the same centuries.

Community life. I use this phrase to capture the odd combination of volunteerism, widespread charitable giving, and engagement in the community that was at the heart of American exceptionalism in the nineteenth century.

The first unparalleled aspect of American community life was the extent of its neighborliness. Neighborliness is not the same as hospitality. Many cultures have traditions of generous hospitality to strangers and guests. But widespread voluntary mutual assistance among unrelated people who happen to live alongside each other has been rare. In the United States through the nineteenth century, it was ubiquitous. Neighborliness refers to the ways residents routinely helped each other out in matters great and small—keeping an eye on a house when its family was away, loaning a tool or the proverbial cup of sugar, taking care of a neighbor's children while their mother was running errands, or shoveling the snow from an elderly neighbor's walk. Neighborliness has often been identified with small towns and rural areas, and there's no doubt that the most dramatic forms of neighborliness—barn-raisings, for example—occurred in the parts of the country where communities were most completely on their own. But the United States developed a parallel tradition of close-knit urban neighborhoods, with identities so strong that their residents defined themselves by the neighborhood where they grew up—South Boston, Flatbush, and Harlem are twentieth-century examples.

The second unparalleled aspect of American community life was vibrant civic engagement in solving local problems. Sometimes this meant involvement in local government, but even more often it was conducted within the voluntary associations that Americans formed at the drop of a hat. Tocqueville saw these voluntary associations as one of the most completely exceptional aspects of American life. A famous passage in *Democracy in America* begins with Tocqueville's observation that "Americans of all ages, all stations in life, and all types of dispositions are forever forming associations." He goes on:

> There are not only commercial and industrial associations in which all take part, but others of a thousand different types—religious, moral, serious, futile, very general and very limited, immensely large

and very minute. Americans combine to give fêtes, found seminaries, build churches, distribute books, and send missionaries to the antipodes. Hospitals, prisons, and schools take place in that way. Finally, if they want to proclaim a truth or propagate some feeling by the encouragement of a great example, they form an association. In every case, at the head of any new undertaking, where in France you would find the government or in England some territorial magnate, in the United States you are sure to find an association.[27]

What Tocqueville saw in the 1830s was just as obvious to Max Weber when he visited the United States at the beginning of the twentieth century: "It has been a characteristic precisely of the specifically American democracy that it did *not* constitute a formless sand heap of individuals, but rather a buzzing complex of strictly exclusive, yet voluntary associations."[28]

The scope of these voluntary associations by the end of the nineteenth century and reaching into the first decades of the twentieth has been largely forgotten. Perhaps this will give you an idea: when Iowa mounted a food conservation program in World War I, it engaged the participation of 9,630 chapters of thirty-one different secular fraternal associations. It is a number worth pausing over: 9,630, in one lightly populated state.[29]

Other nations have had active voluntary associations. The United Kingdom in particular has had a similar civic culture of philanthropy and associations, though functioning differently in important ways because of the English class system. But in terms of scope of activities, the sheer numbers and memberships of associations, and their impact on national history, America's secular non-governmental activism in promoting education, cultural resources, assistance to the poor, and social justice from the Founding onward has no counterpart in the history of any other nation.

The American characteristic that underwrote its community life was an exceptional level of social trust. Social trust means that people assume that strangers they meet are generally trustworthy, helpful, and fair. It has been crucial to America's success, and baffling to other nationalities, who historically have been astonished by the openness of Americans. To them, Americans seemed almost childlike in their trust in the good faith of any random person they came across. In the first half-hour after meeting a total stranger, an American was likely to confide personal information and ask personal questions that might require years of friendship before they would be raised between Europeans or Asians. That same trust made it easy and natural for Americans to do voluntary good deeds, whether on their own or as members of associations—they assumed that their good deeds would be reciprocated somewhere down the road.

EXCEPTIONAL POLITICS

The first use of the specific phrase *American exceptionalism* is attributed to Joseph Stalin, of all people. A prominent American Communist, Jay Lovestone, had argued in 1927 that the advanced capitalism of the United States would prevent the communist revolution from taking place here.[30] Marxism-Leninism could not admit the possibility of such a deviation from the inexorable laws of history, of course, and so Stalin duly denounced "the heresy of American exceptionalism" in 1929. Lovestone had identified a baffling aspect of the American story that has been a major topic among twentieth-century historians and political theoreticians.

Described in broad strokes, the history of politics in Western Europe is an evolution from liberalism to social democracy—*liberalism* used in its original meaning, which is the opposite of the contemporary meaning of liberalism. Liberals of the eighteenth and nineteenth centuries advocated laissez-faire economics and limited government under democratic rule—the politics that originated in America—as distinct from conservatism in public policy and a heavy hand for the state in economic policy.[31] Liberalism saw its first expression in the development of an English liberal party, whose members were known as Whigs, that dominated British politics in the nineteenth century.

Starting around the 1830s and accelerating in the 1840s, Western European nations saw the growth of workers' movements that usually began as demands for the vote, improved working conditions, and the right to unionize. Workers' movements then adopted the socialist framework first developed by French thinkers and brought to maturity by Karl Marx and Friedrich Engels. A tangled history ensued in which socialism and communism competed on the Left, with communism victorious in Russia but not in Western Europe. The countries of Western Europe instead developed an ideological mix of socialist and capitalist thought that became known as *social democracy*. By the 1950s, social-democratic parties were either the dominant or one of the two most dominant parties in the United Kingdom, Scandinavia, the Low Countries, Germany, Austria, and France, and eventually in Greece, Italy, Spain, and Portugal as well.

Social democracy is the ideology of the advanced welfare state, which consists of a combination of democratically selected representatives, extensive state regulation, and cradle-to-grave government programs intended to increase economic equality and buffer citizens from the ups and downs of the economic cycle. Ultimately, the political success of social democracy in the twentieth century is owed to the development back in the nineteenth century of major political parties that were rooted in working-class issues and attracted class-conscious support among members of the working class.

And therein lies another aspect of American exceptionalism: the United States, uniquely among the countries of the West, never developed a strong working-class party. America had an active union movement from the 1820s onward that became powerful in the last part of the nineteenth century and continued to gain strength through the first half of the twentieth century. But the most famous union leader, Samuel Gompers, and the union he led for forty years, the American Federation of Labor, were militantly in favor of more union power but not more state power. Gompers himself was vocally anti-socialist. Until the 1930s, long after working-class movements had become ascendant in Europe, American unionism and political movements remained remarkably divorced from one another.

The reasons why America failed to follow either the predictions of Marxism or the experience of

Europe have been analyzed in an extensive literature that is summarized in Martin Lipset's *American Exceptionalism.*[32] The explanations are in large part consistent with the descriptions of American ideology and American traits you have already read here. Americans did not live in a class-conscious culture. Accordingly, the concept of class-consciousness never took hold here—something that Marx and Engels themselves eventually acknowledged about America. Whatever the reasons, the simple fact that America never developed a workers' party is seen by many scholars of the Left as the most striking aspect of American exceptionalism.

MORE CRITICAL VIEWS OF AMERICAN EXCEPTIONALISM

At the beginning, I said that American exceptionalism does not imply American excellence or superiority, and yet I have described the exceptional American ideology and Americans' exceptional traits in largely noncritical and sometimes explicitly positive ways. That is a reflection of my own perspective as a liberal of the nineteenth-century variety, meaning that I subscribe to the founding ideology of the nation. I also believe that America's historic civic culture was a great achievement and the best environment for enabling human flourishing that the world has yet produced. It is time to summarize the positions that are held by other people, including most European intellectuals and probably the majority of American professors teaching introductory political science and sociology courses, who take a critical view of American exceptionalism.

Slavery and Indians. The positive descriptions of American exceptionalism ignore slavery and the subsequent oppression of African Americans after they were freed. The exceptional American traits existed in distorted forms, when they existed at all, in the slaveholding states. The positive descriptions of American exceptionalism also ignore three centuries of American history during which invading whites pushed Native Americans off their land and exterminated whole tribes from one end of the country to the other.

Ideology. The Founders' passion for limited government and individualism was misplaced. That vision has been overtaken by the more mature, compassionate, and just ideology of social democracy. America should not be struggling to hold onto the remnants of its exceptional ideology but struggling to free itself from them.

Industriousness. Europeans are right when they say that "Americans live to work, while Europeans work to live." Americans are obsessed with money, possessions, and power. Europeans take time to smell the roses. The idea of self-reliance neglects all the ways in which people fail in the marketplace for reasons that are not their own fault. Americans' historic glorification of industriousness and self-reliance are defects in the American civic culture, not virtues.

Egalitarianism. Whatever Americans may say about the equal dignity of all human beings, material inequality in America is far greater than in Europe. American egalitarianism is all about rhetoric, not concrete measures to equalize material well-being. The traditional unconcern of most Americans about economic inequality is evidence of American moral backwardness.

Religiosity. Intelligent people gave up the superstitions of religion long ago. Europe, which is effectively a secular continent except for Muslim immigrants, is more advanced than America in this regard. The continuing vitality of religion in America is a force for reactionary policies, not a force for good.

Community life. Nostalgia has made American community life look better than it was in practice. Voluntary organizations and neighborliness and philanthropy existed side by side with widespread poverty and human suffering of all kinds. Apart from that, most of those community activities were boring, the closeness of community was suffocating, and the reliance upon neighbors for charity was humiliating. It is much more efficient and less demeaning to use the government's social services to provide for human needs than to rely on private charities. It is to Europe's credit that the role of communities has been weakened, and America would be improved by following Europe's lead.

These examples do not exhaust the criticisms of American exceptionalism. Among other things, many people around the world and many American intellectuals are not fond of the American personality. In their opinion, Americans are too chauvinistic, too sure of themselves, too boisterous, too materialistic, too oblivious to the opinions of others. But in this as in all critiques of American exceptionalism, one must distinguish between the opinion of the elites and everyone else.

From the beginning, the masses—first in Europe, later in Asia, and finally in Africa and Latin America—have thought of America as the land of opportunity and flocked to America by the millions. Even today, an American abroad who interacts with ordinary people is likely to be surprised by their affection for and fascination with America. But over those same two and a half centuries, the tone of elite opinion, especially in Europe, has not changed much. The European upper classes and the intelligentsia tended to think from the beginning that America was vulgar, naive, and a little barbaric. By and large, they still do.

3

IS THE UNITED STATES STILL EXCEPTIONAL?

The short answer is that America is still exceptional to some degree, but a lot less than it used to be.

AMERICA'S EXCEPTIONAL SETTING

Just about everything that was exceptional about America's setting has changed. The Atlantic and Pacific oceans no longer buffer us from the rest of the world. Our northern and southern borders do not have to be defended against military invasion, but they now must be guarded against terrorists and illegal immigration. The frontier has not existed for more than a century. As the American welfare state has expanded, the risks of immigrating to the United States and starting from scratch that once were such an effective mechanism for selecting people with unusual determination have been eroded. Ironically, the immigrants who most closely fit the traditional American profile are illegal immigrants, who often must undergo severe hardships and physical risks to get into the country.

AMERICA'S EXCEPTIONAL IDEOLOGY

The Founders had a range of views about how strictly the ideology of limited government should be applied. Some, called the Anti-Federalists, thought that even the original Constitution gave the government too much power. Alexander Hamilton was at the other extreme, arguing that the federal government should undertake improvements of transportation infrastructure and create a national bank. But even Hamilton based his positions on a strict definition of "public goods" (he was, it must be remembered, one of the two leading authors of the defense of the Constitution, *The Federalist*).

The common understanding of the limited role of government that united the Founders, including Hamilton, are now held only by a small minority of Americans, who are considered to be on the fringe of American politics. The Founders retain their historic stature, with both liberals and conservatives quoting snippets of their writings and arguing that the Founders would be on their side if they were alive today. But as a matter of historical accuracy, it cannot be argued that the Founders' views of the proper scope of the federal government bear any resemblance to the platforms of either the Democratic or the Republican Parties.

The expansion of government can be measured in many ways, from the number of people who work for government to the number of laws and regulations that have to be obeyed. But perhaps the simplest measure of the movement away from the Founders' conception of limited government is the monetary size of government. Except for wartime, the federal government never spent more than 4 percent of GDP in any of the 140 years from the founding until 1931. As of 2011, the government spent about 25 percent of GDP.

AMERICAN TRAITS

Over the last fifty years, an American civic culture that once embraced almost everyone has deteriorated. Some specifics:

Industriousness. Americans still work longer hours than Europeans, but the proportion of American working class males in the prime of life, ages 30–49, who worked forty hours a week or more dropped from 81 percent in 1960 to 64 percent in the beginning of 2008 (before the 2008 recession began). The percent of that same group who were not even in the labor force rose from 5 percent to 13 percent during that period.[33] These numbers have no precedent in a country where, until the last few decades, it was taken for granted that all adult males in the prime of life who were not completely disabled would be working or looking for work.

Egalitarianism. Americans still respond to pollsters' questions by saying that they are in the middle or working classes, not the upper class or lower class, but their behavior has changed. Fifty years ago, the American elite consisted of people who had become successful and wealthy over the course of their adult lives, but who overwhelmingly came from modest backgrounds—they were the sons and daughters of farmers, factory workers, craftsmen, school teachers, and the owners of shops, who grew up in small towns or modest neighborhoods in big cities. Even the most elite neighborhoods were not that elite. On the Upper East Side of New York in 1960, famous as a place where rich people lived, the median family income in 1960 was just $55,000 (in 2010 dollars) and only 23 percent of adults had college degrees. By 2010, median family income on the Upper East Side was more than three times its 1960 level, at $187,000, and 79 percent of all adults had college degrees.[34] That pattern applied to elite neighborhoods across the nation. Today, living in an elite neighborhood does indeed mean living in an environment that is highly distinctive from mainstream America, culturally as well as economically. The people who rise to positions that qualify them for the American elite increasingly grew up in these elite neighborhoods, attended elite schools, and have never had personal exposure to life in mainstream America.[35]

Community life. Political scientist Robert Putman wrote a best-selling book called *Bowling Alone* that documented a steep fall in social capital—the social scientists' word for neighborliness and civic engagement—beginning in the 1960s and continuing through the time he was writing the book in the late 1990s.[36] That decline has continued in the twenty-first century, but it now appears that the long-term losses of social capital have been concentrated in working-class America. Community life in traditional upper-middle-class neighborhoods still seems to have many of the attributes it has always had, and there are some indications that new forms of social capital fostered by the Internet are increasing. But among the working class, civic and social engagement in the community have plummeted.[37]

Even more worrisome, social trust has plummeted. The General Social Survey reveals that the fraction of upper-middle-class Americans who agree that most people can be trusted dropped from 71 percent in the 1972 and 1974 surveys to 55 percent in the surveys conducted during 2006–2010. In the middle class, that fraction was 57 percent in the early 1970s, dropping to 38 percent in the surveys conducted during 2006–2010. In the working class, that fraction was already low in the early 1970s, 38 percent. In the surveys during 2006–2010, it was only 20 percent.[38] A high level of social trust was crucial to America's exceptional community life. It has deteriorated among all Americans but most of all in the working class.

Religiosity. Americans still profess a belief in God and attend church far more frequently than Europeans, but secularization has increased substantially. The first decline in religiosity came in the 1960s and 1970s, as the proportion of Americans who said that religion was "very important" to them fell from 70 percent in 1965 to 52 percent in 1978, and weekly church attendance as reported to the Gallup Poll fell from 49 percent in 1958 to 42 percent in 1969, an unprecedented change in such a short period.[39] Then the 1990s brought another major reduction in religiosity, as the percentage of people who said they had no religion at all increased from 8 percent in 1990 to 14 percent in 2000 and increased again to 18 percent by 2010.[40]

POLITICS

America remains exceptional insofar as it still does not have a major political party with a working-class base. The Democratic Party, once America's closest approximation to a labor party, has actually become less identified with the working class since the 1980s, when many blue-collar workers voted for Ronald Reagan and subsequently shifted permanently to the Republicans. American political rhetoric also remains exceptional. Mainstream American conservatives have been much more committed to free-market economics and traditional values regarding family and religion than are mainstream European conservatives. Mainstream liberals have framed their objectives in distinctively American ways, avoiding the language of class warfare and emphasizing traditional American themes of opportunity and upward mobility.

In terms of governing agendas, the distinctions between America's and Europe's politics have blurred. Republican presidents from Dwight Eisenhower through George W. Bush, with the single exception of Ronald Reagan, governed in ways that are similar to those of Europe's center-right leaders. Democratic presidents since Franklin Roosevelt have advocated policies that are generically similar to those of a European social-democratic party.

4

CONCLUSION

The current state of American exceptionalism cannot be captured solely through the measures I have presented. There are many ways in which the typical American personality is still recognizable around the world. America still attracts more immigrants than any other country. America still has the world's largest economy, its armed forces enjoy unchallengeable military supremacy, and American democracy still gives its citizens more direct power to affect government policy than do most other democracies. America continues to transfer power peacefully across administrations and continues to abide by the Supreme Court's interpretation of the Constitution.

But the exceptionalism has eroded. That erosion would not have surprised the Founders. As Benjamin Franklin left Independence Hall on the final day of the Constitutional Convention, a woman asked him, "Well, Doctor, what have we got? A republic or a monarchy?" Franklin replied, "A republic, if you can keep it."[41] His answer epitomized the views of all the Founders. In the course of designing the Constitution, they had systematically studied the experience of every republic that had ever existed, so that their creation could resist the forces that had destroyed them. But they were under no illusions that their solutions were foolproof. They all knew that the political system they had created was fragile.

> *"America still has exceptional aspects, but we are no longer the unique outlier that amused, amazed, and bemused the rest of the world from its founding through the first half of the twentieth century."*

Half a century later, young Abraham Lincoln, just twenty-eight years old, stood before the Young Men's Lyceum of Springfield, Illinois, and gave the address that first brought him to public attention. His topic was "The Perpetuation of Our Political Institutions." In it, he reflected on the prospects of maintaining the American experiment. America was in no danger of being conquered from abroad, he observed, but at the time he spoke, 1838, the nation was facing a new environment. Until then, "the noblest cause—that of establishing and maintaining civil and religious liberty"—had been sustained by the living presence of the generation that fought the Revolution. But by 1838, all but a handful of them were dead. "They were a fortress of strength," Lincoln told his audience, "but what the invading foeman could never do, the silent artillery of time has done; the leveling of its walls."

The silent artillery of time has been at work for many generations since Lincoln spoke. America still has exceptional aspects, but we are no longer the unique outlier that amused, amazed, and bemused the rest of the world from its founding through the first half of the twentieth century. Which of the changes that have diminished American exceptionalism are gains to be applauded? Which are losses to be mourned? Thinking through your answers to those questions is one of your most important duties as an American citizen. Only after you have reached those answers can you know what you want for America's future.

ENDNOTES

For sources that are no longer under copyright and can be found in full on the Internet, I have not supplied page numbers because there are so many editions of such books with different pagination. For the context of the citation, searching on words from a quotation or keywords from the discussion in the text will quickly take the reader to the right place.

[1] The power of judicial review was anticipated by the framers of the Constitution but explicitly became part of constitutional jurisprudence with *Marbury v. Madison* in 1803.

[2] E.g., Newt Gingrich, *A Nation Like No Other: Why American Exceptionalism Matters* (Washington, DC: Regnery Publishing, 2011).

[3] E.g., Tony Smith, *America's Mission: The United States and the Worldwide Struggle for Democracy* (Princeton, NJ: Princeton University Press, 2012). Thomas Jefferson saw America as having a special role in this regard, referring to the United States as "the sole depository of the sacred fire of freedom and self-government, from hence it is to be lighted up in other regions of the earth," but he did not have foreign wars in mind as a way of lighting up those other regions. Quoted in Merrill D. Peterson, *Thomas Jefferson and the New Nation* (New York: Oxford University Press, 1970), 920.

[4] E.g., Godfrey Hodgson, *The Myth of American Exceptionalism* (New Haven, CT: Yale University Press, 2009); and Brian T. Edwards and Dilip Parameshwar Gaonkar, *Globalizing American Studies* (Chicago: University of Chicago Press, 2010).

[5] For a discussion of the Founders' view that a successful republic required a high level of virtue in the people, see Charles Murray, *Coming Apart: The State of White America, 1960–2012* (New York: Crown Forum, 2012), chap. 6.

[6] Thomas Jefferson, First Inaugural Address, 4 March 1801.

[7] Frederick Jackson Turner, *The Frontier in American History* (New York: Henry Holt and Company, 1921).

[8] Ibid.

[9] Quoted in Seymour M. Lipset, *American Exceptionalism: A Double-Edged Sword* (New York: W.W. Norton & Company, 1996), 18.

[10] Letter to Henry Lee, 8 May 1825.

[11] This discussion is drawn from Charles Murray, *In Pursuit: Of Happiness and Good Government* (New York: Simon and Schuster, 1988), chap. 8.

[12] James Madison, *Federalist* 51.

[13] Alexis de Tocqueville, *Democracy in America*, vol. 2, part 2, chap. 8, trans. Henry Reeve (New York: Adlard and Saunders, 1838).

[14] Bernard Bailyn, *The Ideological Origins of the American Revolution* (Cambridge, MA: Belknap Press of Harvard University Press, 1967), 319.

[15] Francis J. Grund, *The Americans in Their Moral, Social, and Political Relations*, vol. I (Boston, MA: Marsh, Capen and Lyon, 1837).

[16] Henry Adams, *History of the United States during the First Administration of Thomas Jefferson*, vol. 1 (New York: Charles Scribner's Sons, 1889).

[17] Thomas Hamilton, "Men and Manners in America," *Frasier's Magazine for Town and Country*, vol. 9, no. 159, January 1834.

[18] Grund, *The Americans*.

[19] Alexis de Tocqueville, *Democracy in America*, vol. 2, part 2, chap. 4.

[20] Letter to the officers of the first brigade of the third division of the militia of Massachusetts, 11 October 1798, in *The Works of John Adams, Second President of the United States: with a Life of the Author, Notes and Illustrations, by his Grandson Charles Francis Adams*, vol. 9 (Boston, MA: Little, Brown, and Company, 1856).

[21] Letter to Dr. Benjamin Waterhouse, 26 June 1822.

[22] Lipset, *American Exceptionalism*, 63.

[23] Ibid.

[24] Michael Novak, personal communication. For a full discussion of religion's role in the American founding, see Novak, *On Two Wings: Humble Faith and Common Sense at the American Founding* (San Francisco: Encounter Books, 2002).

[25] Lipset, *American Exceptionalism*, 63. Readers who want to explore the interplay between religion, the American character, and political reform movements should read David H. Fischer, *Albion's Seed: Four British Folkways in America* (New York: Oxford University Press, 1989).

[26] Robert W. Fogel, *The Fourth Great Awakening & the Future of Egalitarianism* (Chicago: University of Chicago Press, 2000).

[27] Tocqueville, *Democracy in America*, vol. 2, part 2, chap. 5.

[28] Max Weber, *The Protestant Ethic and the Spirit of Capitalism* (Mineda, NY: Dover Publications, 2003).

[29] Theda Skocpol, *Diminished Democracy: From Membership to Management in American Life* (Norman, OK: University of Oklahoma Press, 2003), 63–4.

[30] Donald E. Pease, "Exceptionalism," in *Keywords for American Cultural Studies*, ed. Bruce Burgett and Glenn Hendler (New York: NYU Press, 2007), 108.

[31] Lipset, *American Exceptionalism*, 31.

[32] Ibid., chap. 3.

[33] Murray, *Coming Apart*, 272–73.

[34] Author's analysis of the 1960 Census and the 5-year American Community Survey for 2006–2010.

[35] Murray, *Coming Apart*, chap. 1–3.

[36] Robert D. Putnam, *Bowling Alone: The Collapse and Revival of American Community* (New York: Simon & Schuster, 2000).

[37] Murray, *Coming Apart*, chap. 14.

[38] Author's analysis, General Social Survey.

[39] Robert D. Putnam and David E. Campbell, *American Grace: How Religion Divides and Unites Us* (New York: Simon & Schuster, 2010), chap. 4.

[40] Author's analysis, General Social Survey.

[41] Max Ferrand, ed., *The Records of the Federal Convention of 1787*, vol. 3 (New Haven, CT: Yale University Press, 1911), appendix A, 85.

ACKNOWLEDGMENTS

My thanks go to Christopher DeMuth, Steven Hayward, Gertrude Himmelfarb, and Michael Novak for their terrifyingly erudite reviews of the draft and the many improvements they inspired.

Charles Murray is the W. H. Brady Scholar at the American Enterprise Institute. He first came to national attention in 1984 with *Losing Ground*. His subsequent books include *In Pursuit, The Bell Curve* (with Richard J. Herrnstein), *What It Means to Be a Libertarian, Human Accomplishment, In Our Hands, Real Education*, and *Coming Apart*. He received a bachelor's degree in history from Harvard and a Ph.D. in political science from the Massachusetts Institute of Technology. He lives with his wife in Burkittsville, Maryland.